5

Simple

Practices

for a lifetime of joy

AMAYA PRYCE

Cover and Interior Design:
John H. Matthews, bluebullseyepress.com

Cover image: © Can Stock Photo Inc. / blue67sign

*This book is dedicated with love and
gratitude to Shahn McGuire, mentor and
counselor extraordinaire.*

TABLE OF CONTENTS

INTRODUCTION
Shortcut to Nirvana

Row, row, row your boat gently down the stream.
Merrily, merrily, merrily, merrily,
life is but a dream.

What does a nursery rhyme have to do with Nirvana? More than you might think.

First, let's define Nirvana. For me, it means "heaven on earth." It means living life with a baseline of joy, peace and well-being. It doesn't mean you don't have any problems, because let's face it, that's life, and learning is what we're here for. It means having a deep inner sense that everything's going to be all right, no matter what's going on around us.

It sounds pretty good, doesn't it? I've been looking for it for a long time, getting glimpses, following tracks, heading into cul-de-sacs, even occasionally turning in the wrong direction altogether. It often felt like hard work and – the dreaded word – discipline. That's where the nursery rhyme comes in. Maybe it's not supposed to be that hard.

Imagine this: what if Nirvana is what we're supposed to experience? What if it's as easy as gently drifting downstream, enjoying the view?

I know. That sounds great, but you're totally not buying it. We're conditioned from an early age to think that we have to work hard to achieve any important goal, but I invite you to just set that belief down for the length of this book. Take a deep breath. Relax your shoulders. There's an easier way, I promise.

When I first started to look seriously for "enlightenment," I read every book I could get my hands on (roughly half a zillion) and began signing up for classes and trainings like the über-diligent seeker I was. I tried everything short of the shamanic-journey-with-psychedelic-plants route, although I even gave that some thought. I had a spiritual To-Do list as long as my arm, stretching from morning pages to meditation, gratitude journals to mindfulness practice to vision boards to binge watching Super Soul Sunday. I was a spiritual junkie.

Fortunately, sanity gradually prevailed. I slowly began to notice that, in spite of the huge variety of teachings and the confusing array of techniques out there, it all mostly boiled down to a handful of basic practices. These five practices – which I call Notice, Feel, Question, Connect and Love – appeared over and over in the books I read, although they were described in different terms and supported by very different ideologies.

Once I recognized these common threads, my spiritual practice became a whole lot simpler and more enjoyable... not to mention more fruitful. And this is what I'd like to offer you. It's the Cliff's Notes version of all the reading and study I did and, though it might not be a "shortcut" to Nirvana, at least it's the most direct route I know of.

Each of the five practices is a small mental shift or course correction that, practiced over time, can change the trajectory of your whole life. None of them is complicated or difficult or time-consuming. Anyone can use them: Christian, Jew, Buddhist, atheist, pantheist, you name it. They are completely portable. You can even practice them right in the midst of daily life and no one will know (well, they'll know because you'll look so serene and happy).

The five practices build on each other, but you don't have to use every one of them every time (and certainly don't try all the techniques all at once, or you'll be burned out in no time). We're just playing here. Remember the feeling of floating gently downstream? There's a reason they're called "practices." It's not a performance. There's no right way to do them, and no way you can do them wrong. Doesn't that feel better already?

One final note: This book is intended to be a primer of sorts, an introduction for those new to this genre, and a refresher for old hands. Almost all of the concepts and techniques I describe here have been written about before, often in many different forms, by many different authors. When I'm aware of where I first heard an idea expressed, or expressed in a unique way, I've made a great effort to credit that source. You'll find the titles of many books from my favorite authors referenced throughout (and a reading list at the end), so I hope you'll be inspired to dive in even deeper. My very sincere apologies if I've inadvertently failed to give credit where it's due.

And now... Nirvana and a lifetime of joy are waiting, so let's get started, okay?

Ready. Set. Relax.

THE PRACTICES
1. Notice

To live is so startling as to leave little time for anything else.
~ Emily Dickinson

The utterly simple practice of noticing is the basis for every positive change in life. Twelve Step programs recognize that no one can overcome a problem until they're willing to admit that they *have* a problem. Unconscious habits, ingrained thoughts, repetitive and unhelpful patterns of behavior; none of them can be changed until they're brought into conscious awareness.

And noticing problems is only half of this powerful practice. There's also noticing the riches of the senses: the feel of fresh, clean sheets, the smell of coffee, the taste of chocolate, the sight of a full moon climbing into the sky.

To take delight in something, you first have to notice it. Same for feeling gratitude. Almost every aspect of life can be heightened, deepened, and made more meaningful simply by paying attention to it.

To notice is to be mindful, aware, awake, conscious. You might not realize this, but the power of your attention is one of the most potent forces you have at your disposal. It's like a high-beam flashlight, illuminating and energizing whatever you focus it on. Martha Beck says, "Your life follows your attention. Wherever you look, you end up going." Deepak Chopra says, "Attention is important, because whatever you pay attention to grows."

Attention is powerful, especially when you wield it with *intention*. Often we don't. Often what gets our attention is the latest crisis popping up, or the slight we think the boss gave us in today's meeting, or the five pounds we gained this month. Not things we really want to expand. Learning to intentionally direct your attention to the positive pays off in the short-term (because it's more pleasant to focus on the things that make you happy) and in the long-term (because expanding those good things will most likely make you even happier).

But as good as that sounds, it gets even better. We're going to turn the flashlight of your attention onto a part of yourself that you might never have met before, at least consciously. I call it the Observer. This is not the voice in your head that yells at you when you do something it considers stupid, or serves up a constant barrage of opinions and alarms as you go about your day. We'll talk about that voice – the mind – in Chapter 3. The Observer, on the other hand, is all about non-judgment and compassion.

When you think about yourself, who's doing the thinking? Right now, you're thinking about yourself thinking about yourself. However many layers you go back, there's always a presence behind the last thought that's doing the thinking. Who is that entity? It's "you" and yet separate from you at the same time, since "you" are also the object of the thinking.

Do you ever find yourself laughing at something you've done? Not in a mean way, but just gently laughing at your own foibles? Who's doing the laughing? There's a quality of acceptance and good humor in this entity that I don't find in my normal mental chatter. The mind bullies and shames and directs, while the Observer just sits back and watches it with a smile. The classic Zen illustration is this: the baby (you) watches the toy (the physical world), but the mother (the Observer) doesn't watch the toy, she watches the baby. The mother knows that the toy isn't what's important; it's the baby. And yet she also doesn't judge the baby for going after the toy. That's the nature of the baby.

The Observer is the constant presence witnessing all the activity of your mind and body. *Presence* is an interesting word, meaning both an "entity" and the act of being present in the here and now. It's the opposite of absence, as in absent-minded, as in multi-tasking, as in autopilot. Buddhists call it mindfulness. We'll just call it noticing.

Gateway Drug

If the practice of noticing is the "gateway drug" of sorts to enlightenment, then breathing is the gateway drug to noticing. Paying attention to the breath is probably *the* number one technique you'll encounter if you study the self-help liturgy. This used to drive me crazy, because there are few things in life I find less stimulating than watching my breath going in and out, in and out, ad nauseum. Unfortunately, that's sort of the point.

Breathing ties you to the present moment, and (fortunately for us) it's always going on. It's also a convenient blend of voluntary and involuntary, which lets us play around with it when we want but doesn't require us to. Conscious breathing is the fastest, most reliable way to ground and calm yourself in stressful situations. When your heart is pounding and you're flooded with anxiety, frustration or anger, try taking several deep, slow, deliberate breaths. This activates the parasympathetic nervous system, which is the mellow counterpart to the fight-or-flight, sympathetic nervous system. It will calm your heart rate right down and let you get back to more important issues, like digestion and making good choices.

And that, my friend, is about as complicated as it gets. First, you notice that you're getting stressed out, and then you notice your breathing and consciously slow it down. Simple, but amazingly effective – provided you actually do it. I can be somewhat impetuous, and conscious breathing has saved me from many an unfortunate reaction. Watching the breath is a classic technique for meditation, which we'll talk about in Chapter 4, but it can easily be slipped into little mini-sessions throughout the day, whenever you want to feel more grounded and present.

Another stealth mindfulness technique is to simply pay attention to the way your feet feel on the floor (or your bum on the chair, your hands on the steering wheel, and so on). This is especially useful when your mind is spinning in place, worrying about the future or reliving the past. Use your body to bring yourself back to the present moment. Try it now. Just concentrate on that part of your body – shine your flashlight there – and feel what you feel. Hard, soft, rough, smooth. What's the temperature? Are your clothes or shoes tight or comfortable? What else do you notice? See how much information you can take in. And then ponder how much information you regularly ignore.

Of course, we have to be selective with our attention, or we'd never be able to deal with the millions of bits of information that come at us each second. The point of mindfulness is to be *aware* of where we're focusing. Basically, it's choosing the subject of our attention consciously rather than randomly (whatever pops up on the screen) or automatically (whatever we've simply become accustomed to focusing on).

It might come as a surprise to realize that you can choose the subject of your focus. Most of us are so used to following our well-worn mental and behavioral ruts that we've come to believe they're virtually set in stone. ("Of course I have to think about my ex-husband/boss/mother-in-law/landlord. If I didn't, who knows what they'd do next?") This is where noticing comes in handy. And the Observer.

The Observer

The really great thing about the Observer is that it never judges us. It just nods, makes a note and then lets it go. That's it. And that's all it takes to set the process of change in motion. The wonder of noticing is that, just with the act, things have already begun to shift... maybe only a little at first, but then gradually gaining momentum, until eventually you're clear of the ruts and setting a new course of your own choosing.

It's pretty close to magic, and it all starts with bringing conscious awareness to bear on every part of your life: feelings, thoughts and actions. And this powerful source of energy – your attention – interacts with and changes the physical world in ways that quantum physicists are only beginning to understand. Science has proven that the simple act of observation affects the behavior of subatomic particles – and that means you, me and everything else in the universe.

I won't go into great detail here (mainly because I can't), but there's a wonderful layman's discussion of quantum physics and its implications in the book *What We Talk About When We Talk About God* by Rob Bell. He writes, "Matter is ultimately energy, and our interactions with energy alter reality because we're involved, our world an interconnected web of relationships with nothing isolated, alone, or unaffected."

I've come to see this as the principle of "grace" in action. When you try to break a bad habit or introduce a good one through sheer force of will (the ego), it never seems to work. Maybe for a while, but eventually you'll let your guard down and before long you're right back where you started, with an extra helping of defeat thrown in. But when you bring simple awareness to a behavior or thought pattern, it begins to change automatically. Not all at once, and usually not dramatically; but slowly and surely, if you continue to just notice consistently, you'll find yourself changing (almost) without effort.

According to Lama Surya Das in *Buddha Is as Buddha Does,* "It doesn't matter whether we suffer from a short attention span, a quick temper, weak willpower, a compulsion to lie, an addiction to drugs, or a habit of zoning out in front of the TV or numbing ourselves with booze or food. Our basic inner-self alertness..., all on its own, can do wonders to nip the problem in the bud."

Let me give you an example. In the past, I tended to be very critical of others, and I probably let them know my opinions a little too often. This is something I wanted to change, for obvious reasons. I had tried sternly correcting myself many times before, but it never seemed to stick for long. As I learned to be an observer of myself, I began to simply notice how often a critical thought crossed my mind. I wasn't really trying to stop them, but was just interested to see them popping up. Then I started to name the thoughts, like this: "Hmmm... disapproving again." And that's about it.

Eventually, by some lovely alchemical process – grace – I found that not only was I making fewer critical remarks, I was even having fewer critical thoughts. The Observer's non-judgmental awareness seemed to create a space between the thought/behavior and me. Rather than being a "critical person," I was just a person having the occasional critical thought, which felt a whole lot easier to deal with than attempting a complete personality makeover.

This illustrates one of the main problems with unconscious thought and behavior patterns. Because we aren't consciously aware of them, they begin to feel like an innate part of us, as in: "I can't help it, it's just the way I am." When you learn to step back and view them objectively, they start feeling less like a life sentence and more like what they really are: just a choice, and one that you can always do differently next time. Awareness brings with it the power to choose your response, while unconsciousness flips on the autopilot switch.

The gift of the Observer is to create breathing room and a much-needed sense of proportion around a situation or problem. The mind loves nothing better than making dire, all-or-nothing pronouncements, but you can simply thank your mind for its input and then politely ignore it. Imagine that you're a scientist studying a fascinating natural phenomenon. Try mentally labeling your thoughts or behavior when you notice them (such as "procrastinating" or "judging"). Just stay as objective and non-judgmental as you can, no matter how much your mind wants to go into blaming and shaming mode. It won't happen overnight, but gradually we're going to wrest control from that well meaning little despot and put the benevolent Observer in the driver's seat. (And yes, the mind is well-meaning, if misguided. More on that in Chapter 3.)

Nothing Doing

Your inner scientist can also help when using the next technique, which is probably the simplest but most powerful of all. Martha Beck, one of my all-time favorite authors (*The Joy Diet*, *Finding Your Own North Star* and others), calls it "body whispering." She says that our bodies, like horses, are basically prey animals that have been terrorized by the bullying mind. To gentle them, like a horse whisperer gentles a horse, she suggests spending fifteen minutes every day simply doing nothing.

This is harder than it sounds, and in fact I did it faithfully for several weeks before I began to really reap the benefits. The object is simply to tune in to your body, exploring your inner and outer sensations like a scientist, or an alien finding itself in a human body for the first time. What makes it frustrating is that most of us are so out of tune with our own bodies that we wouldn't recognize a sensation if it bit us on the nose (well, maybe then).

You might even find, when you check in, that you're actually kind of numb. Start with just your big toe, and try to inhabit that fully. What do you feel against your skin? How does it feel on the inside? If you have to, wiggle it up and down some. Then work your way up your body all the way to your head. When doing a body scan like this, pay special attention to the abdomen, chest and neck, where unresolved emotions often hang out. (This will be great practice for Chapter 2.) You can do it in any position, even lying down, as long as you can keep from falling asleep.

It's simply a process of becoming reacquainted with your body and learning to notice what it's telling you. The body is speaking all the time; we just don't listen. There's a nexus of nerve tissue in the intestines called the enteric nervous system (or, more inelegantly, the gut brain) that may be the physiological origin of the famous "gut feeling." Eventually you'll become re-attuned to the point that you'll instantly know when it's trying to get your attention. The body becomes a trusted friend again when you learn to deliberately vacate your head for a while.

In this sense "mindfulness" is a deceptive term, since it seems to imply being more in the mind, when actually the opposite is true. Far from the fog of mental channel surfing that normally fills my head (news commentary/static/songs I never want to hear again/static/long harangues on the soapbox of your choice/staticstaticstatic), I find a few moments of crystal clarity coming through on the line. It's a blessed relief that can become quite addictive.

This is the mental state that many sports – especially dangerous ones – foster, and I suspect it's the real reason people practice them. Clinging to a sheer rock face 500 feet up a cliff, where your next handhold is the difference between life and death, probably also reduces mental chatter... but I feel compelled to point out that there are easier ways to accomplish this that involve no technical equipment whatsoever.

You can practice mindfulness in the safety of your own living room by simply tuning in to the sensory experiences of sight, sound, smell, touch and hearing. There are many classic meditations available on how to eat or walk mindfully, including Jon Kabat-Zinn's twenty-minute meditation on letting a raisin dissolve in your mouth (I'm serious). Sometimes it's fun to isolate each sense and concentrate solely on what you hear or smell or feel. Slowly and mindfully performing a familiar task like washing dishes or brushing your teeth can ground you in the present moment and reveal sensual pleasures you usually pass right by.

In all these techniques, you'll find yourself drifting in and out of mindfulness, but don't judge yourself when that happens. Just gently bring your attention back, however many times it wanders. Perfecting the technique isn't the point. The Buddhist teacher Adyashanti wrote, "I have found that often, if we are not careful, these ancient traditions and techniques... become an end instead of a means to an end. People end up with what is simply a discipline. They end up watching their breath for years and years and years, becoming perfect at watching their breath. But in the end spirituality is not about watching the breath."

It's the same trap I fell into earlier in my spiritual quest. The techniques point you in the right direction, but they aren't the destination itself. The destination, in this case, is waking up. But come on, I hear you saying, I'm already awake. You should see how much I get done in one day! I know: your eyes are open, your mind is racing and you are the king or queen of productivity. How can you possibly be asleep?

Waking Up

The hectic pace of modern life is deceptive. It may seem like we're wide-awake and productive, but in reality most of us sleepwalk (or run) through life. It's been estimated that 90% of the thoughts you have today are identical to the thoughts you had yesterday. Now that's a scary thought. We let the culture in which we live set our priorities and values for us. We look to celebrities and the media to dictate fashion and acceptable behavior. We forget who we really are in the constant pursuit of who we think we should be. We've lived unconsciously for so long, we almost don't believe there's another way to live.

How did this happen? Small children, like animals, live in the present moment, alive to the world, both inner and outer. As they grow older, and especially when school enters the scene, the ego develops protective mechanisms for dealing with peers and social demands. This isn't entirely a bad thing; to live and work in close community with others does require some compromise and conformity for the benefit of the group. However, the ego rarely stops with that. Gradually, as the mind and social norms gain more and more power, the inner knowing of the body and the compassionate awareness of the Observer are pushed aside. We essentially become addicted to one aspect of ourselves: the tyranny of the mind.

As with any form of addiction, the beginning of a cure is awareness, the specialty of the Observer. You can't solve a problem you don't know you have, so the first step is always simply to notice. Just look around your life and see what you see. What's good in it? What works? It's always best to start with the positive.

Make a list, in your head or on paper, of all the things, little and big, that are right in your life. When you want to build something new, the best foundation to build on is gratitude for where you are right now. It's so easy to become mired in regret and self-condemnation, especially if you, like me, are coming to this process later in life. The past decades can seem like a colossal series of mistakes, but I firmly believe that we couldn't be going through this process now if we hadn't experienced every one of them. Give yourself credit for all that you've learned along the way. Remember what Maya

Angelou told Oprah: "When we know better, we do better." That's a relief.

As you look around (and especially when you start looking at what doesn't work in your life) the attitude you want to cultivate is curiosity, not judgment. Remember, the hallmarks of the Observer are always compassion and non-judgment, so when the urge to judge rears its ugly head, you'll know that the ego is back on the job. And don't beat yourself up when that happens either… judging yourself for judging yourself will only send you down an endless rabbit hole.

We're being gentle with ourselves, remember?

Once you get clear on what's working and what you'd like to change, you know what to do. Notice, take delight in, feel gratitude for all the good. Then shine the light of your attention into the dark spaces and begin to gradually release the thoughts and behaviors that no longer serve you. It's as simple as that.

Checking In

Well, we've made it down the first stretch of the stream. I really hope you were able to relax a bit and enjoy the scenery as it glided past. On the next stretch we'll be taking these observational skills and applying them to your emotions. So take a deep breath and get ready to explore a world both richer and more joyful (and occasionally scarier and sadder) than you may have experienced before.

THE PRACTICES
2. Feel (your feelings)

...our lives are mostly a constant evasion of ourselves.
~ T.S. Eliot

If there's one thing that most people get "wrong" (including myself for about five decades) it's emotions. We mix up thoughts with emotions. We think feelings just happen; that they're beyond our control. We label some feelings good and other feelings bad. And worst of all, we don't know what to do with them: we try to suppress them or run away from them, and then inevitably end up acting them out in some inappropriate way. Or else they make us sick.

I've been guilty of all of these. The irony is that emotions are, literally, our friends. And not just the good ones. Feelings are simply a built-in guidance system we were born with to help us navigate our way through life. It's like a giant game of "hot and cold," with emotions providing the feedback. We spend so much time and effort trying to escape from or manage something that simply needs to be noticed. Once you get the hang of it, your emotions will become your most trusted allies, you'll get sick a lot less often, and people will be amazed by how much calmer and happier you are. You will too, I promise.

First, let's make sure we're all on the same page. In this chapter I'm going to use the terms "feelings" and "emotions" interchangeably. And by feelings, I mean something you actually feel in your body, not something you think in your head. When you ask someone how they feel about something, they'll often respond with a thought. "I feel like he should apologize to me" is a thought. The feeling behind that thought might be anger, or hurt, or both. "I'm bored" might really be a feeling of sadness or loneliness.

Just remember, feelings are energy, and they're located *in the body*. You can even think of the word "e-motion" as "energy in motion." The main thing you need to remember is that emotions cause physical sensations: a racing heart, heaviness in the chest, butterflies in the stomach, tightening in the throat, and so on. We're so used to living in our heads and ignoring our bodies, I'm guessing that I'm not the only one who had thoughts and feelings thoroughly mixed up. For the record: we'll get to thoughts in the next chapter. Right now, it's all about the body.

Loving Kindness

In the body whispering exercise, we started getting reacquainted with that shy animal, the body. I find this whole process akin to coaxing a terrorized cat or dog out from under the bed. It takes patience, a soft voice and massive doses of self-kindness. The first thing I'd prescribe is a steady diet of Loving Kindness meditations. To do this, place one or both hands over your heart and silently say, "May I be well. May I be happy. May I be free from suffering." Repeat until you feel a sense of peace and relaxation. This has become a very profound practice for me, and one that I continue daily (many times a day, as a matter of fact).

If you're as clueless as I was about emotions, you may not have any idea how to go about "feeling your feelings." Or you may think that you're doing a fine job of emoting, when what you're actually doing is just rehearsing your stories (thoughts) over and over. The first time I really understood the difference was when a man stepped in front of me at Starbuck's and placed an order for his entire office building. I felt a very distinct, hot sensation flood my chest and throat, and I was so intrigued that I sat down right then to examine it. I had plenty of time, after all.

The trick at this point is to disengage completely from your thoughts and just focus on the sensations. I didn't sit there and stew over the guy's jerky behavior, or how unaware the Starbuck's employee was not to have noticed that I was next in line. Of course, I could have just said something, but this was too good an opportunity to miss. The funny thing is, when you actually concentrate on feeling your feelings intensely, they don't last very long! Ninety seconds. That's what Jill Bolte Taylor discovered when she had a stroke that knocked out the verbal processing part of her brain (see her book *My Stroke of Genius: A Brain Scientist's Personal Journey*). When you don't keep telling yourself the story over and over, emotions are actually processed very efficiently.

To help the process along, try getting back into scientist mode. Dr. Russ Harris, in his book *The Happiness Trap*, recommends making the sensations bigger and even "surfing" them, in a sense. Once I had my breakthrough experience in Starbuck's, I was off on a roll. For practice, let's imagine that you're lying in bed, feeling anxious. You notice a fluttering, buzzing sensation in your stomach and chest, which previously you would have either ignored or tried to reason yourself out of. It probably seems counter-intuitive to make that unpleasant feeling even bigger, but humor me here.

Imagine yourself expanding to hold the sensation as it grows, as if you're creating a container for it. You might find that you're bracing yourself and holding your breath when you do this, so remember to relax and keep breathing slowly and deeply. Most of us have been told our whole lives that strong, uncomfortable emotions should be avoided at all costs, so you're bucking a lifetime of conditioning.

Keep focusing on the physical sensation and try to describe it in words. Where is it, exactly? What "color" is it? Does it move around? Does it change? Check your whole body (hands, legs, jaw) for sensations. For now, do your best to leave the story of why you're feeling that way alone and just stay with the experience until it dissipates. Afterward, jot down a description, or you can even draw a little diagram. The purpose is to learn your own body's emotional language, so that you can recognize and interpret it more accurately in the future.

Try to be as specific as you can in naming it. This is trickier than it might seem at first glance. Sometimes I honestly don't know what I'm feeling, and sometimes two emotions, like fear and excitement, can show up in similar ways in the body, even though they have very different messages. If you can't pin it down, go for the broad categories – mad, sad, glad and scared – and then try to narrow it down from there. You can find very long, detailed lists of emotions on the Internet if you need some suggestions.

Tolerating Discomfort

And that is the basic practice of feeling your feelings. Since most people are already quite happy accepting their "good" feelings, it will probably be the difficult ones that most need your attention. It's worth talking here about how uncomfortable we are with feeling uncomfortable. Really, we'll go to extreme lengths to avoid it. We'll make ourselves sick avoiding it. And is it really all that bad? I started asking myself that question while reading Pema Chödrön's book *When Things Fall Apart*. She writes: "Generally speaking, we regard discomfort in any form as bad news. [...] Most of us do not take these situations as teachings. We automatically hate them. We run like crazy."

"Running" can take the form of suppression or of acting out, but always it's a way to resolve tension that feels unbearable. Forms of suppression (distraction) include eating, drinking, channel surfing, working long hours, shopping, watching kitten videos on YouTube... anything to numb out and avoid those uncomfortable feelings. When running takes the form of acting out, it will be some reflexive, reactive behavior that usually doesn't serve you well. For instance, I get uncomfortable in some social situations and can end up over-talking or over-sharing in an effort to feel like I fit in and am liked. Afterward I feel inauthentic and embarrassed.

Ask yourself: what would happen if you didn't run? What if you just got curious instead? Start with something small. I made a quick post in a Facebook group recently that I almost immediately felt uncomfortable about. My urge was to take it off as quickly as possible, but then I decided to just see if I could tolerate the discomfort and investigate the feeling (there's the scientist again). I realized that I was sabotaging myself with unfounded worries of what "everyone" would think. When I gave myself time rather than fleeing into reflexive action, I realized that the post was perfectly appropriate, and my discomfort disappeared like magic.

My therapist calls this "holding onto yourself." It's the ability to simply tolerate anxiety, uncertainty, doubts and other uncomfortable feelings long enough to figure out what's really going on, instead of leaping into evasive maneuvers or trying to force a premature resolution (which rarely works).

It can help to look at emotional pain as you would physical pain. If your back or knee started hurting, you might at first ignore it or try aspirin and rest, but if the discomfort continued or worsened, you probably wouldn't continue to simply overlook it. You would want to find out what was causing it, and what you could do to solve the problem, right? You're not ashamed of having a sore knee. You don't think it makes you look weak or "bad." It's just a sore knee. You'd take care of it without a second thought.

Emotional pain is no different; it's just a signal your body gives you that something needs your attention. Running from it might temporarily ease the pain, but when it comes back it's usually much worse (and it will keep getting worse until it forces you to pay attention). Next time you feel sad, angry, lonely, anxious, and so on, try to catch yourself in the act of running, whether that means numbing out or acting out. Instead, experiment with simply feeling the discomfort. Concentrate on the sensation in your body. When I do this, it's almost laughable how easy it is to tolerate sensations I've spent years running from.

A side benefit of this practice is that it puts you squarely in the present moment of your experience. When we try to escape from the "negative" emotions, we're essentially numbing out from our lives and what's really happening in them, the good along with the bad. If you aren't willing to experience the lows, eventually you become less capable of enjoying the highs as well. The poet Rainer Maria Rilke even wrote this: "Were it possible for us to see further than our knowledge reaches, and yet a little way beyond the outworks of our divining, perhaps we would endure our sadnesses with greater confidence than our joys."

In the end, life is full of ups *and* downs. This is duality in practice, and since it's what we came here to experience, we might as well embrace it. Contrast is essential to the learning process, and also to simply savoring what it is to be human. Experiencing sadness helps you truly appreciate happiness, just as a cold drink tastes best when you're really hot and thirsty, and sleep is pure bliss when you're bone-tired.

The Good, the Bad and the Transformative

Not that I'm expecting you to like feeling bad, just to tolerate it long enough to really get the message it's bringing. Making judgments is a quintessential human quality, pretty much impossible to avoid. In fact, you can and should use your ability to discern what feels good and bad as a litmus test for making decisions in life. Martha Beck calls this idea the "body compass." Basically, when you're heading in the right direction your emotions (body, remember, not mind) will be saying, "Yum!" When you're heading in the wrong direction the message will be "Yuck." It's as simple as that.

The important thing is to stay out of your head. Not that you can't use your analytical powers at all (that would be silly), but when you're tuning in to your body compass, focus only on the bodily sensations. There's room for both thoughts and feelings in making decisions, but don't confuse one with the other. All of the work you put into body whispering and noticing emotions will pay off nicely here. Even subtle differences indicate "warmer" or "colder" messages: any improvement in your feeling state will feel lighter and freer in your body (expanded), while the reverse will feel heavier and more restrictive (contracted). The more you tune in and practice listening and acting on the feedback you get, the more finely calibrated your body compass will become, and the better you'll get at navigating toward your own best life.

Of course, this can be dangerous if you're attached to not making changes in your life. You might find that certain people and activities consistently make you feel like you're hoisting a ton of bricks. This is a clear indication that they aren't serving your highest good… but then you will have to figure out what, if anything, to do about that. Fortunately, your body compass will guide you there as well. Just hold an idea or thought in your mind and check out the feedback from your body. Is it Yum or Yuck? Hotter or colder?

Another good way to visualize and work with your feelings is to see them as a kind of emotional ladder that you can work your way up, from the lowest rungs (hopelessness and despair) through anger (yes, anger is an improvement over despair) and boredom, to contentment, excitement and, ultimately, joy/love/freedom/gratitude/etc. This process was outlined by a group of "non-physical entities" called Abraham, and channeled through a lovely woman named Esther Hicks. I recommend her book *Ask and It Is Given,* if the supernatural factor doesn't bother you.

Abraham explains that every emotion has a certain vibrational frequency, which makes sense if you think of emotions as energy. The better-feeling emotions vibrate at higher frequencies. If you believe in the so-called Law of Attraction (I do), vibrating at a higher frequency attracts people and events that "match" that frequency and will bring you even more joy/love/freedom, etc.

I used to get a bit bogged down at this point. Seemingly, we'd want to spend all of our time in those higher vibration, better-feeling places, which contradicts the whole notion of tolerating discomfort and not running from the "bad" feelings. The trick is to fully acknowledge and feel where you are first. If you try to leap directly to joy without doing the inner emotional work, you will rarely be successful. This is sometimes called "spiritual by-pass" and it's similar to pasting a smiley face over a problem rather than actually fixing the underlying cause. Unfortunately, there aren't many Get Out of Jail Free cards handed out in the Game of Life.

(Er…Monopoly.) It's more often a case of "pay me now or pay me later."

Shadow Work

Which brings me to a subject that I love: the Shadow. We'll be covering this more in Chapter 5, but it's also very pertinent to any discussion about emotions. All those uncomfortable feelings that we push aside or repress don't just politely take themselves elsewhere. Nosiree, Bob, they just set up camp in the body and hang out, causing mayhem from time to time until they're finally acknowledged and processed. In fact, they can basically shanghai your body without warning and go on a spree that will leave you shaking your head, apologizing and sometimes even writing out reparation checks.

Eckhart Tolle calls these unprocessed negative emotions the pain-body. In *The Power of Now* he writes: "It has two modes of being: dormant and active. A pain-body may be dormant 90 percent of the time; in a deeply unhappy person, though, it may be active up to 100 percent of the time. Some people live almost entirely through their pain-body, while others may experience it only in certain situations, such as intimate relationships, or situations linked with past loss or abandonment, physical or emotional hurt, and so on."

As with any shadow, the way to deal with it is to bring it into the light (consciousness). The pain-body "feeds" on negative emotion and loves to create even more drama, for you or anyone else handy. Unconsciousness creates it, while awareness dissolves it. I like to imagine the happiness-sucking dementors from the Harry Potter books, which can only be dispelled by a Patronus charm. Once you become aware of the pain-body's existence, it has a much harder time lulling you back into unconsciousness. When you feel it waking up – and you'll soon learn to recognize that downward spiral of negative thoughts and emotions – you only need to notice and name it to stop it in its tracks.

Better yet, in Chapter 5 we'll learn how to actually befriend the disowned parts of us that lurk in the shadows. We expend tons of psychic energy keeping them hidden, so there are many benefits to letting them out into the light of consciousness. There's a heavy price to pay for burying emotions like anger or grief, and often it's paid in terms of physical illness. As with the practice of expanding emotions, it may seem counter-intuitive (and even foolish) to actually look for these long-buried feelings. Shouldn't we just "let sleeping dogs lie?" That might work if they'd actually keep on lying, but they won't. Better to wake them up and deal with them consciously than to step on them in the dark and get bitten.

In *The Dark Side of the Light Chasers*, Debbie Ford writes: "Search around for stored up anger. If you are fearful about discovering your anger, remember that your power is buried along with it. Anger is only a negative emotion when it is suppressed or dealt with in an unhealthy way." Every emotion, whether it's stored up from long ago or in response to something happening right now, comes with a gift for you. Anger, for instance, is often about the need to set boundaries. Karla McLaren's classic book *The Language of Emotions* contains a brilliant discussion of these gifts and messages.

Another reason to bring suppressed emotions into awareness is that they often contain clues to long-time, unhealthy behavior or relationship patterns. None of your emotions is random or useless. Even when something seems "out of the blue," trust that there is a meaning and a message behind it. Stay with it and gently feel around. It might lead you back to a long-forgotten incident that was never properly mourned or acknowledged. Often these incidents are from childhood, when we didn't have the wisdom or experience to understand or put them in perspective.

Maybe it was the time your mother accidentally drove off and left you in the gas station restroom on I-90 (true story). Years later, you might still get a little strident or panicky whenever someone isn't where they said they'd be. Give yourself permission to feel those feelings now. If it helps, do a Loving Kindness meditation for the scared child in you, and maybe one for your poor distracted mother, too. Bring in the Observer. When you find a stash of old anger or sadness or fear, just feel it (and you know how to do that now). "Processing" is just a fancy word for noticing, and noticing, as we know, has a magic way of unraveling even the snarliest of problems.

Befriending Your Emotions

Keep on peeling back the layers, because uncovering buried emotions is rarely a "one and done" situation. Eventually you'll greet those emotions like long-lost friends, which they are. Let them guide you. Listen to what they tell you. Get to know the way they feel in your body. They're here for you, including the uncomfortable ones (maybe even especially the uncomfortable ones). Bring them into your conscious awareness, and they'll work for you rather than against you.

In the next chapter we'll bring the same practice of noticing to your thoughts, although here our goal is to question, rather than accepting them at face value. With the Observer at the helm, the body and mind can learn to work together for your highest good, like two oars pulling smoothly in the same direction. This will make rowing down the stream a whole lot easier (and merrier).

For inspiration, I'll close with my favorite poem by the 13th century Persian poet Rumi, which beautifully illustrates this open, accepting relationship:

The Guest House

This being human is a guest house.
Every morning a new arrival.

A joy, a depression, a meanness,
Some momentary awareness comes
As an unexpected visitor.

Welcome and entertain them all!
Even if they're a crowd of sorrows
Who violently sweep your house
Empty of its furniture,
Still treat each guest honorably.
He may be clearing you out
For some new delight.

The dark thought, the shame, the malice,
Meet them at the door laughing
And invite them in.

Be grateful for whoever comes,
Because each has been sent
As a guide from beyond.

THE PRACTICES
3. Question (your thoughts)

There is nothing either good or bad, but thinking makes it so.
~ Shakespeare

Our approach to the mind will be very different from the way we dealt with the body. The mind (ego) is used to calling the shots, being in charge, keeping us on our toes. And thank God for that. We might not even get out of bed in the morning if it weren't for that tireless – and tiresome   dictator, cracking the whip. I know my daughter wouldn't.

We had to coax the body out of hiding, flush our feelings out into the open where we could see and acknowledge them. Not so with thoughts. Thoughts are always, always with us: yammering   away   non-stop,   whispering, directing, correcting, sometimes literally yelling in our mental ears. Buddhists call it "monkey mind." It's definitely like living in a zoo.

Byron Katie (she goes by just Katie) was forty-three when she woke up one morning on the floor of a halfway house for eating disorders and found that she could no longer believe her thoughts. She still had them, of course, but they no longer seemed like "her." The truth is that thoughts themselves aren't really the problem; it's the fact that we identify with our thoughts. We think they *are* us and (here's the kicker) we think they're true.

Are they true? Can we absolutely know they're true? These are the first two questions Katie learned to ask about any thought. And, it turns out, there are really very few things we can absolutely know are true. We make assumptions about everything: what people are thinking, what their motives are, what might happen in the future, why something happened in the past, and on and on. You might think you know the answers, but can you actually be sure? Do other people know exactly what your thoughts and motivations are?

So, let's say you have a thought about some person or situation that you think is true. Maybe it's: He shouldn't have left me. Or: The government can't be trusted. How does that thought make you feel? Probably not very good. It probably doesn't contribute a whole lot to your happiness or peace of mind. I wonder what it would feel like if you didn't have that thought? I know… this part is a stretch. Can you even imagine what it might feel like if you could just choose not to have a thought that causes you pain? Because you can.

"The Work"

Byron Katie's book *Loving What Is* describes the process of questioning thoughts that she calls The Work. It's a bracing read for most of us non-enlightened beings. In fact, almost everyone initially kicks back pretty hard against the notion that we can choose our thoughts and (horrors!) that they might not even be true. That's the identification I was talking about. If you feel resistance to the idea, you have "bought in" to your mind's story. Welcome to the club.

We are story-telling machines. We have a story about everything, and many of them are quite useful. You have a story about who you are, what your childhood was like, how the world "works." I have stories about what my purpose on Earth is, why people do what they do, whom I can or can't trust. Every person and thing and event in your life has a story. Some of your stories came from your parents or teachers or friends, and some of them came from your own experience of the world. No two people have the exactly the same stories, even about the same events, so how can anyone's stories possibly be "right" or "wrong" in the absolute sense?

If you need proof of that ask your siblings, if you have them, to describe some of their memories of your shared childhood. They might remember the same bare-bones events you do, but their interpretations and feelings about those events will likely be different (sometimes startlingly so). You don't have to give up your stories, and it probably wouldn't be possible anyway, but just being aware that they *are* stories is the first step toward freedom from unconsciously identifying with them. They belong to you, but they are not you. And are they true? Can you absolutely know that they're true?

The process for doing The Work of Byron Katie can be summed up in a little jingle: "Judge your neighbor, write it down, ask four questions, turn it around." Because it's pretty much the gold standard for working with thoughts, I'm going to describe it in some depth here, but I strongly encourage you to study her writings yourself. She has a great website (www.thework.com) with many resources and videos of herself doing this work with all kinds of people on a whole range of topics.

The most satisfying part of the process is filling out a "Judge Your Neighbor" worksheet (you can download these on her website), because this is where you get to let loose and really say what you think: what someone has done to you that they shouldn't have done, what they haven't done that they should have, and exactly how you feel about it. You're encouraged not to try to be all enlightened when doing this, because the purpose of the worksheet is to discover exactly what you do think, not what you think you should think.

After that it gets gnarly. Taking one thought at a time, you ask the following questions:

1. Is it true?

2. Can I absolutely know that it's true?

3. How do I feel/act when I think this thought?

4. Who would I be (how would I act) if I didn't have this thought?

It's best to take your time in answering, so that it becomes almost a meditative process. I find that this is especially important with the third question, because that's where the discomfort that we talked about last chapter comes in. Usually we don't want to dwell on those unpleasant emotions: anger, jealousy, betrayal, powerlessness, the desire for revenge, hurt, grief, loss. Sounds like a great party; who wouldn't want to go? But this is precisely where the healing is.

You dive into the emotions and hold them up, one at a time, to the Observer. And remember what the Observer brings to the party: non-judgmental compassion. If you can stay in that place of acceptance and listening, your body will serve up some amazing insights, guaranteed. At the very least, you'll have an opportunity to acknowledge and process some painful emotions that otherwise might trip you up in other ways (illness, acting out, self-sabotage). Be sure that you really feel them, as we practiced in Chapter 2. Pay very close attention to the sensations in your body. At best, you'll discover the ways that you are contributing to the problem, which is great news, since you're the only person you can change.

Be careful not to rush ahead to the fourth question prematurely. This is a great example of spiritual by-pass, especially tempting to people who have done The Work for a while. We know we're "supposed" to be able to disbelieve our painful thoughts, so we rush the process to get to the feel-good, enlightened part, before we've fully acknowledged and processed the uncomfortable feelings. Unfortunately, I've tried it and it doesn't work.

If you haven't done The Work before, you might not even understand *how* to answer the last question. What do you mean, "who would I be?" And how can I make myself not believe something I do believe? It takes an imaginative leap, but try it. Just think: if I woke up tomorrow morning and I just didn't have this thought, how would my life be different? What would I do differently (in the same situation) if I somehow got selective amnesia and couldn't think this thought? As you imagine that, see how it feels in your body. How is that sensation different from the sensations you felt in question 3?

Turn It Around

The final part of The Work completes the bending of your mind into a pretzel. You take the original thought and "turn it around" in certain prescribed ways: first to the opposite, next to the self, and finally to the "other." If that sounds like gibberish, let me demonstrate. Let's say your original thought was: He shouldn't have left me. Here are the turnarounds for that thought:

1. He *should* have left me. (opposite)
2. *I* shouldn't have left me. (self)
3. I shouldn't have left *him*. (other)

Now, does that still sound like gibberish? I thought so. Before you give up in disgust, remember that the point of this exercise is simply to gain a little detachment from the hold your thoughts have on you. Katie always says, "And you don't have to change that thought; you can keep it if you want." The turnarounds simply give you a chance to see if there might be some truth in a different story than the one you've been telling yourself. We're just looking for a little wiggle room here, like loosening a tooth. Ask yourself: is it possible that this new statement is true in *any* way? Try to come up with three "pieces of evidence" that it might also be true.

For instance: He should have left me.

1. Well, if he wasn't happy, then he should have left me. If he was my brother and he was unhappy in a relationship, I would have wanted him to leave it.

2. In some ways, I am better off now that he's left.

3. (Digging deep) Maybe I needed to learn something important from this experience that I couldn't learn any other way.

Finding pieces of evidence to support turnarounds can be very challenging and frustrating, but it's worth the effort. Depending on your original thought, you might not always be able to do all three turnarounds. And remember, you don't have to give up your original thought; it's just a way to detach from your story a bit and at least entertain the possibility that other stories might have some validity as well.

I have to admit, this process is not for sissies… but you've probably figured that out for yourself by now. It's a bit like lancing a boil to release the toxins: fascinating in a painful kind of way, but extremely satisfying once it's over.

Thought Work

If you're too squeamish to tackle The Work just yet, don't give up hope. There are other good methods of inquiry. The main ingredient in all forms of thought work is simple awareness, our old friend. Remember, you can't change a problem unless you know that you have one. The most important decision you can make is simply to choose to pay attention to your thoughts. They matter! Marcus Aurelius said, "The happiness of your life depends upon the quality of your thoughts."

Most people, most of the time, aren't consciously aware of what that persistent voice in the mind is saying. It's been our constant companion ever since we had words to use. Martha Beck coined a great term to describe a very common habit: story fondling. We actually fondle our stories, trotting them out to look at and exclaim over and discuss, over and over again. You know you do this! I certainly do. And if it's a horror story, all the better. Everyone likes a good horror story, right?

The basic question to ask yourself is: how does that story (or thought) make me feel? If it makes you feel good, then keep it. If it makes you feel bad, question it. Find a better-feeling story. You get to be the narrator of your life, so why not choose to tell an epic adventure, or a heady romance, or an inspiring morality tale (or all of the above)? Why saddle yourself with horror stories and boring dissertations? What's the pay-off?

Because there's always a pay-off: something that you get in return for the sad story, whether it comes from yourself or from other people. Pity. Camaraderie. Black humor. Righteous indignation. An excuse for why your life isn't going the way you wish it was. Whatever it is, I guarantee it's not as fun or exciting as actually being the hero or heroine of your own kick-ass life. And all it takes (really) is telling a different story. Try it now. Take a story in which you've cast yourself as the victim, and retell it as a heroic adventure. There are still dragons and challenges in fairy tales, or else they'd be pretty boring, but the protagonist always triumphs in the end, stronger than before. You can be that kind of protagonist.

Dragons and challenges on the outer level may be intimidating, but it's the ones on the inner level – thoughts and beliefs (which are just thoughts that you've had for a long time) – that can really mess you up. In *Self Coaching 101*, Brooke Castillo writes, "My thoughts were painful – but I didn't know this. I thought it was my life that was painful. I didn't see that I needed to change the thoughts in my mind – I thought I needed to change my life." Change, as you often hear in the world of therapy, is an inside job. It's a lot more fun to try to change everyone else, but 1. It doesn't work, and 2. No one will thank you for it. I've tried that, too.

Castillo's method for identifying and changing painful thoughts involves tracking the progression from outer *circumstances* (which you usually can't change) to the *thoughts* they trigger, which then cause *feelings*, which prompt *actions*, which lead to *results* (which will inevitably produce evidence that reinforces the original thought, whether it was positive and helpful or negative and self-defeating). The point at which you can most effectively intervene in this progression is at the level of thought.

The circumstance is what it is. (Engrave that on your brain. Tattoo it on your forearm.) When you consciously look for a better-feeling thought about it instead of fruitlessly gnashing your teeth over it, it changes the whole cascade of reactions, from feelings to actions to results. And here's the best part: if you do this consistently, and consistently experience better results as a consequence, it becomes a virtuous cycle. And we like virtuous cycles. So much better than those negative ones.

Whose Business Is It?

Byron Katie has a useful way of looking at this. When you're trying to shift the responsibility for your thoughts and feelings onto someone or something else (the circumstance), she will ask, very sweetly, "Whose business are you in now, honey?" By her reckoning, there is my business, your business and God's business, and the only one that we have the right (or ability) to influence is "my business." This gets to the heart of both responsibility and boundaries.

Responsibility for your thoughts, feelings and actions always rests with you, and only you. You choose your reactions, every time. That's often hard to accept, but the good news is that it works the other way around too. Yes, you have 100% responsibility, and no less. But also no more. You are NOT responsible for anyone else's thoughts, feelings and actions. That's their business. And God's business is everything else.

It's very simple, but most of us don't maintain very sturdy boundaries. We like to get into other people's business, and we often tolerate them getting into ours. And all of us think we know what God should do. The poet Robert Frost wrote, "Good fences make good neighbors." Healthy boundaries work two ways, keeping others out of your business and reminding you when you've strayed into theirs. Simply asking yourself the question "Whose business is this?" is usually enough to re-establish the boundary.

As in every other case we've discussed, awareness is the key to change. Awareness of when you give your power away to someone or something else, or allow someone to take your power away. If you're accustomed to feeling powerless it might be intimidating to realize how powerful you actually are. There's comfort and familiarity in victimhood.

If you're accustomed to fixing and managing everyone else (this was my particular vice) it can be scary to let them go off on their own to possible failure and heartache. Or even to competence and success, without you. My therapist uses a helpful phrase here: "Let them have their own experience." I'm now on a mission to change my personal equation from loving = helping to loving = letting go. It's also scary to stop living *through* other people and realize that you've been conveniently neglecting your own growth for a long time. There's comfort in playing the role of rescuer too.

Welcome to the world of healthy boundaries! It may not be as comfortable, but it's a lot more interesting and fun, I promise. And now...

A Word About Words

In his book *The Four Agreements*, Don Miguel Ruiz writes, "The word is the most powerful tool you have as a human; it is the tool of magic." (Spoken metaphorically, of course.) In urging us to be "impeccable" with our words, he emphasizes the power they have to work both good and ill in the world. While unconscious thinking is mostly harmful to ourselves, unconscious words allow us to spread that harm far and wide. Nearly everyone remembers some thoughtless pronouncement from childhood that continues to sting well into adulthood.

The responsibility (and privilege) of choosing your thoughts wisely goes double for words, but each has its own challenges. Thoughts are insidious because, as we've seen, we're often totally unconscious of our thought patterns (though not anymore, right?). Words "concretize" thoughts, which makes them easier to spot – but it also gives them even more power, for better or worse.

I'm especially convinced that the words we say about ourselves are taken as virtual marching orders by the subconscious. If you're in the habit of saying things like "I always get a bad cold this time of year" or "I'm so stupid about technology," then stand by to have those words become your actual, on-going experience. Abraham agrees with me here: "Nothing else in your experience responds as quickly as your own physical body to your patterns of thought."

This is a good place to talk about affirmations, which are a great idea often gone wrong. To be effective, affirmations – which are just positive statements that you deliberately "program" into your subconscious – have to be believable. The reason this is true is that, when you tell yourself something that you can't really buy (maybe something a bit too grandiose, like the classic "Every day, in every way, I'm getting better and better"), your mind immediately rejects it and undoes whatever good you were hoping to accomplish.

It's not that you can't be grandiose; you just have to be able to *believe* it for it to work. Better to work your way up to grandiosity step by step. If you want to love your body but you currently can't stand to look in the mirror, start with "I love the way my hands look" or "I really appreciate my body for all that it can do." You'll know that you've hit on a good affirmation because it will give you a sense of relief and lightness. (Remember the body compass? Perfect for this situation.) An affirmation that isn't right will make you feel anxious or discouraged or angry. Tune in to the feedback your body is giving, and you'll find that affirmations actually work quite well.

And while we're on the topic of words, here's another plug for good boundaries: be very, very picky about the words that you "let in" to your psychic space. That is your space, and you get to say what's welcome there and what's not. People will say all kinds of things, but you're not obligated to listen. I always tell my daughter, "Someone can hand you a cup of poison, but it's up to you whether you drink it." I've noticed that we'll sift through a whole litany of compliments in order to find and swallow the tiny bit of poison that's hidden there, even if it's imaginary. So stop it! If you truly want peace of mind, walk away from the poison, no matter how tempting it is.

And finally…

Here's a pop quiz. What's the most important thing you need in order to live a life of joy? Let's say it together: Awareness. Just pay attention to your life, to your actions, to your feelings, to your thoughts.

And then give it some time, and watch things change. You really don't have to stress about it. In fact, if you do, it's probably a good sign that you're letting your ego back in the driver's seat. Henry David Thoreau wrote, "As a single footstep will not make a path on the earth, so a single thought will not make a pathway in the mind. … To make a deep mental path, we must think over and over the kind of thoughts we wish to dominate our lives."

The ego always likes to force things, and it wants them to happen *now*. The Observer works on its own timetable. Often, we just need time to integrate new ideas and put them into practice. There's really no hurry, and rushing the transformative process usually backfires anyway. While the ego uses the force of will, the Observer wields the power of intention. The difference is that with intention there's no strain. No trying to force the boat upstream.

In *Happy for No Reason*, Marci Shimoff gives the following formula for effortless change: Attention – intention – no tension.

So, relax that death grip on the rudder and come with me on the next stretch of the stream. We're more than halfway to Nirvana already.

THE PRACTICES
4. Connect

Let us be silent – so we may hear the whisper of the gods.
~ Ralph Waldo Emerson

Awareness will bring positive changes to every part of your life – thoughts, feelings and actions. This is great news, but it's not by any means the end. As awareness seeps into all the cracks and crevices of your life, transformation inevitably follows. In this chapter we'll explore ways to deepen your connection with the compassionate and non-judgmental Observer, a.k.a. your Higher Self. It's both the source of inner wisdom and joy, and the bridge to an even Higher Source of love and guidance. Sounds like a good deal, doesn't it?

The Higher Self is the part of you that literally takes the higher view of life. The Social

Self, on the other hand, is the persona we normally show the world. The Social Self runs on fear, while the currency of the Higher Self is love. To the Social Self, the world is a competition at best and a war zone at worst. To the Higher Self, it's a playground. The more you can shift your base of operations from the Social Self to the Higher Self, from contracted awareness to expanded awareness, the happier and more peaceful your life will be on every level.

One great way to do that is through a regular practice of meditation. I hear you groaning, but you'll thank me for this later. There are some huge misperceptions about meditation out there that I hope to dispel. One, that it's hard. (It isn't, and I'm 100% sure that you're already doing it in one form or another.) Two, that you have to be either very spiritual or very hippy-dippy to do it. (There's plenty of mainstream research proving the health benefits of meditation for everyone.) Three, it's boring. (Well, this one is kind of true, at least some of the time. But it's still incredibly worth the effort, as I plan to convince you.)

Even if you're really resistant to the idea of a Higher Source, you can still reap all the benefits of meditation and the practice of awareness. For you doubters I recommend the book *10% Happier*, by ABC news anchor Dan Harris. A thorough skeptic, he took up meditation to help him overcome anxiety attacks on the air (gulp) and became a huge fan. He writes: "I suspect that if the practice could be denuded of all the spiritual preening... it would be attractive to many more millions of smart, skeptical, ambitious people who would never otherwise go near it." So there.

Spiritual or not, in this chapter you'll learn a whole plethora of ways besides meditation to "plug in" to the power of consciousness. Awareness is always available to you, instantly. The Observer doesn't go away somewhere when you aren't paying attention to it. In this sense, there's no need to connect to awareness, because you can never really *dis*-connect from it. But you can certainly ignore it, and unfortunately many of us do so quite regularly.

Unconsciousness causes problems, to put it mildly. In *Breathing Under Water*, Richard Rohr says, "No one consciously does evil. The very fact that anyone can do stupid, cruel or destructive things shows that they are at that moment *unconscious and unaware*. [Emphasis his.] Think about that: Evil proceeds from a lack of consciousness." He even suggests that it would be more helpful for people to "examine their consciousness" rather than their conscience. Strong words from a Catholic priest.

So what's the antidote? Anything that gets you out of the constricted, fear-based Social Self and into the larger perspective of the Higher Self. Brother Lawrence, living in a 17th century monastery, called it "practicing the presence of God" (and I'm using the term "God" loosely here, even though he wasn't). According to him, any activity – sacred or secular – can be done with the intention of connecting to God/awareness. The intention is more important than the activity itself, although here are some good places to start: Prayer. Contemplation. Gratitude. Time spent in nature or with animals. Journaling.

Repetitive, soothing activities. Absorbing, fascinating activities. And, yes, meditation.

Demystifying Meditation

I confess that I was a failed meditator for many years. I really wanted to do it; I was convinced that it would be good for me, but I just couldn't stick with any routine. I couldn't make my thoughts go away. And I certainly couldn't sit on a cushion on the floor in lotus position (or even half-lotus) without becoming very cranky, very quickly. It wasn't the result I was hoping for.

I was making the same mistakes many people do when it comes to meditation. The biggest was thinking that I needed to somehow "stop thinking." I'm not sure that's even possible for the Dalai Lama, although I haven't asked him. Thoughts come and go. The only difference is that, in meditation, you try not to hold on to them. And try is the operative word here. You quite often won't succeed, and that's okay. In fact, that's where the real learning comes in, simply from catching yourself running after a thought and calmly starting over. If it were easy to detach from our thoughts, we wouldn't have all the problems we do in the first place.

So instead of aiming for a blissfully clean (and unattainable) slate, think of your mind as an Etch-a-Sketch, with thoughts appearing randomly and then just as randomly disappearing, to be replaced by other thoughts. You just lazily watch the show, without becoming attached to either the thoughts or to the slate being clean. If it helps, you can focus on something else, the most common being your breath or a mantra (a repeated word or phrase). You can even just count to ten in your head over and over. There's no such thing as the meditation police, so do what works for you.

I mix it up all the time, even within one meditation session. Sometimes I watch my breath, sometimes I listen to music or do a visualization, sometimes I say a mantra (usually something simple and tied to my breath, like "In – Out" or "God – Love"). Sometimes I have blissful sessions, and sometimes there's a prison riot going on in my head. Since the idea is not to get attached to results, I just shrug them both off, the "good" and the "bad." Judging is the ego sticking its oar in yet again, so thank it and ignore it. Trust that you're getting exactly what you need.

The thing is, there are tons of different ways to meditate. It's possible that if you go to a fancy meditation retreat, they'll say that you "have" to sit on a cushion on the floor, or you "have" to use a certain mantra. I don't know; I've never been on one of those. I almost always sit in a chair or even lie down to meditate. In general, I'd say that "have to's" miss the whole point of meditation practice, which is to sink into a place of non-judgment and compassion (hello, Observer).

Rest & Play

In her book *Finding Your Way in a Wild New World*, Martha Beck describes an infinity loop of rest and play, like this: "Play until you feel like resting, then rest until you feel like playing." Although she doesn't specifically apply this to meditation, I think it makes a great touchstone for evaluating what might or might not work for you in your practice (and life!). What feels like rest to you? What feels like play? Both of these are gateways to the present moment and expanded awareness.

For some people, driving is a meditation. Or taking a walk, or knitting, or gardening. A long, hot shower or bath can be a great meditation. Sitting on a park bench in the sun (Eckhart Tolle reputedly did this for two years after he became enlightened). Any solo, repetitive, mostly mind-free activity that you enjoy will work brilliantly.

Or, conversely, any pleasurable activity that takes all of your concentration. Rock climbing, a game of tennis or golf, playing an instrument, making art. Anything that fascinates and absorbs your attention so completely that time seems to fly past. This is the phenomenon of "flow," which is supposed to be one of the most pleasurable states we can achieve. Mihaly Csikszentmihalyi, the name-challenged psychologist who coined the term, writes of these optimal experiences: "The best moments usually occur when a person's mind or body is stretched to its limits in a voluntary effort to accomplish something difficult and worthwhile."

Many of these are things you do already without consciously labeling them meditation. Now you can pat yourself on the back and do them even more. Intentionally cultivate feelings of bliss, relaxation, flow and timelessness, and take advantage of every opportunity to bring them into your day. But don't stop there.

Formal "sitting" meditation is still the fastest way I know to cultivate your connection with inner awareness. Try to do it every day, even if only for five minutes. Whatever amount of time you invest will bring great rewards, and longer (when you're ready for it) is better still. Here are some more ways to keep things interesting. Feel free to play!

- When you're observing your breath, try "connected" or "circular" breathing, which is simply trying to connect each breath without pausing in-between. Don't try to breathe more deeply than normal, or you'll hyperventilate. Just focus on making a smooth transition between each inhalation and exhalation.

- Find a "sit spot" outdoors where you can spend twenty minutes quietly observing nature. Make it a regular practice and you'll get to know your wild neighbors and the subtle changes of weather and seasons.

- Once a week, try to stretch out the length of your session. I meet my 82-year-old mother in an empty church each week to sit for an hour. At first the time seemed almost impossible to get through, but now I love these sessions. (And she has lowered her blood pressure by ten points!) We bought an hourglass to mark the time, which is less jarring than a clock or timer.

- Feel free to shift your position if you get uncomfortable; I always have to vary my back position at some point. If you get an itch, try concentrating very hard on the "itchiness" of the sensation and it usually goes away. When I get sleepy I sometimes squeeze my hands together as hard as I can and concentrate on that sensation. Or just let yourself sleep. It may be exactly what you need that day.

- Remember the Loving Kindness meditation? If I'm feeling very upset and having difficulty settling down for meditation, this is my go-to… I once did it for a solid hour after receiving divorce papers in the mail. Just repeat: "May I be well. May I be happy. May I be free from suffering." If you're feeling generous, the Buddhist practice is to go on to say it for others: "May you be well. May you be happy. May you be free from suffering." Start with someone close to you, then someone "neutral" (someone you know, but not well), then someone you have difficulty with and, finally, say it for all beings.

- An especially good beginning meditation is to download a song like the "Devi Prayer," which is twenty minutes long and sung in Sanskrit, so you aren't distracted by the words. You can also meditate to birdsongs and all kinds of nature sounds free on YouTube.

And finally, there are so many ways to use visualizations as part of meditation that they get a section of their own.

Playing with Energy

Visualizations use the power of thoughts and imagination to accomplish a purpose more or less "virtually." The purpose might be relaxation, healing, protection, communication, inspiration, assistance, and so on, for yourself or someone else. (Theoretically you could also use them to do harm, but we won't even go there.) The interesting question is: how much effect do you believe visualization – the energy of thought – actually has on the "real world?" When you visualize, are you actually accomplishing your purpose in reality?

Even if you're not totally convinced that your thoughts have the power to impact physical reality, remember the findings of quantum physics and at least consider "acting as if" they did. Here are a few visualizations to start with:

- For grounding and safety, picture a thick, strong cord coming from the bottom of your feet or the base of your spine, and reaching all the way down to the center of the earth like an anchor. Imagine energy from the core of the earth flowing up through the cord and into your body.

- Picture a bubble of white light (or whatever color you like) surrounding you. Imagine that you can breathe the light in and send it all through your body, into every cell. Concentrate on any area of your body that needs healing.

- If you're concerned about someone, rather than sending them the energy of worry, imagine them instead surrounded by beautiful white light and "send" them love and joy. Surround your home, or your town, or the whole earth with protective, healing energy. This feels a lot better than simply worrying about the state of the world.

- And in case you're tempted to dismiss all of this as New Age nonsense, here's a great visualization courtesy of the Roman philosopher Plotinus: "Let the soul banish all that disturbs; let the body that envelops it be still, and all the frettings of the body, and all that surrounds it; let earth and sea and air be still, and heaven itself. And then let the man think of the spirit as streaming, pouring, rushing and shining into him from all sides as he stands quiet."

There are plenty of guided visualizations available online and in books, and you can always make up others that suit your needs. Experiment with using the power of your thoughts and imagination consciously. In his classic *Think & Grow Rich*, Napoleon Hill wrote: "Imagination is the workshop of your mind, capable of turning mind energy into accomplishment and wealth." (And other good things too… he was a little fixated on money.)

Become aware of the energy you're putting out, and also of the energy you pick up from others. We're much more sensitive to this than we think – and others are too. I used to believe that I could hide my emotions and thoughts from others. Now I know that I'm always broadcasting them loud and clear, whether I want to or not, so I'm careful to keep my energy as "clean" as possible. If you knew that other people were constantly reading your energy (they are), would that change the way you think? It changed me.

More and more, I'm coming to believe that the quality of my intention, or energy, is at least as important as my action – if not more so. Abraham says, "There simply is not enough action in the world to compensate for the misalignment of Energy..." And Meister Eckhart put it this way, centuries earlier: "Visible deeds... can never be worth much if the inward process is small or non-existent and they can never be of little worth if the inner process exists and is great."

Of course, that doesn't mean you shouldn't act at all. Perhaps St. Francis of Assisi said it best: "What is it that stands higher than words? Action. What is it that stands higher than action? Silence."

Inner Dialogue

Prayer is last on my list of techniques that foster connection, because I think that religions often emphasize talking *to* God a lot more than listening for an answer. But dialogue is a two-way affair, and there's certainly a place in any intimate relationship for expressing, questioning, kvetching, revealing, mulling over a problem, or simply sharing a joke. And then balance this with a hefty dose of silence, so that you can hear the reply.

Like meditation, I've had a complicated relationship with prayer. In fact, I've had a complicated relationship with God. Maybe you don't believe at all, or maybe you have a fine relationship with God (and by God I mean whatever you call Him/Her/It). Or maybe you're one of the legions of one-time believers who were scalded by prior religious experiences.

Although that issue is beyond the scope of this book, I can recommend one that was very helpful to me: *Outrageous Openness* by Tosha Silver. If you feel even the smallest urge to re-open the God door and take another look, I think you'll love her joyful take on spirituality. She writes of the Divine as "an energy and an awareness available to anyone, regardless of religious background or beliefs. It's an ever-present Love always waiting inside to guide us in any circumstance… if we request its help."

Though I boycotted prayer for many years, I recently returned to the practice after reading Tosha's book and giving my concept of God a much-needed makeover. Before that, my prayers tended to be formal and verbose, whereas now they're intimate and often wordless. Like Anne Lamott, they mostly consist of: "Help me, help me, help me" and "Thank you, thank you, thank you." Which seems to be enough.

Writing is another way to keep up your part of the inner dialogue. Many people, including Oprah, swear by gratitude journals. So-called "morning pages" are another common practice. I use a website called 750words.com to do a few pages of stream-of-consciousness writing every morning. (They even give you little badges when you have a streak of days going, which is always a plus.) I'm often surprised by what I end up writing. When you do a practice like this consistently, the subconscious will start to use it as a way to get important messages through to your conscious mind. That's how dreams work too, and if you keep a dream journal close to your bed you'll soon find your dreams becoming much more vivid and helpful as well.

Trust

"Helpful" is how I hope you come to see all the workings of your Higher Self, whether that means God to you or simply your subconscious. In a very profound sense, your happiness depends on whether you see the world and its events as inimical to you... or simply random and uncontrollable... or even benign and helpful. Albert Einstein said, "The most important decision we make is whether we believe we live in a friendly or hostile universe." And that guy was *smart*.

Remember that the Social Self views everything from the perspective of fear. The oldest and most primitive part of our brains – the so-called "reptile brain" – is hard-wired to alert us to any perceived danger. While this was once useful, when we had to deal with saber-toothed tigers and hunting down our next meal, its negative bias is now a liability.

The central question to ask yourself is: do things happen *to* me, or do they happen *for* me? It's not just playing with words; it's two completely different philosophies of life. This was a huge shift for me, and I'm still getting my bearings in a world where I'm not constantly preparing for the worst. It had a lot to do with my God makeover, from the toxic God that Julia Cameron describes as "a withholding parent who denies our dreams" to a God who is "a cocreator, a partner, in our dreams."

If I truly believe that everything that happens is meant to happen, and is ultimately for the highest good of all (and I know that I'm skating on thin ice here), then maybe it's possible to not only "accept" what happens, but to actively embrace it. And I won't argue with anyone who says that things happen in this world that should NOT be embraced. But they still happen, whether we embrace them or not. Where I fall on the continuum of responses depends on the day.

I do believe that suffering is actually a choice we make. Not sadness, not grief, not righteous, mighty anger. Open up and let them in. They are all "clean pain," and the only way past them is through them. You have to walk right through the ring of fire till you get to the other side, battered and singed, but whole.

Suffering, on the other hand, is "dirty pain," and it comes from resisting what *is*. In the Bible it's called "kicking against the goads" (a goad is a sharpened stick used to get an animal going in the right direction), which is a powerful image of the pain we cause ourselves by taking a stand against reality. Clean pain – without the resistance – will make you stronger and softer and wiser. Dirty pain makes you hopeless and bitter. There are days when hopeless and bitter might sound perfectly reasonable to you (I know those days), but at some point you're going to want to move on, and that choice will be there for you too.

The novelist Henry James described the challenge this way: "The world is not to be put in order, the world is order incarnate. It is for us to put ourselves in unison with this order." The Social Self, which is heavily invested in trying to put the world into order, does not embrace this attitude easily. It takes a leap of faith to look beyond the world of appearances to the underlying order that already exists, and for that you need the perspective of the Higher Self.

For me, it helps to think of life as a series of "puzzles and games." As a parent, I know that two basic motivations are behind every experience I've tried to create for my daughter: I either want her to learn something or to enjoy herself or, ideally, both. If you accept God as a loving parent and the universe as a friendly place, then every experience you're given can be seen as either a puzzle (something to learn from) or a game (something to enjoy for its own sake).

And the best puzzles are usually challenging! If they're too easy, they're simply boring and you don't learn anything from them. The trick with puzzles (learning experiences) is how willing you are to learn the lesson. I used to believe that all learning involved struggle and pain. I've since chosen to delete that programming. The psychologist Gay Hendricks wrote, "We choose how gently we get our lessons by how open we are to learning."

When you resist the lesson, life just keeps coming back at you with harder and harder puzzles. Martha Beck's excellent advice is: "Cave early!" My new intention is to learn my lessons willingly, with the least resistance possible. If I can learn through joy I'll take that any day, and if pain – clean pain – is the price of learning (and sometimes it is), at least I'll try not to dirty it up by kicking against the goads.

And One More Thing...

Whether you're currently grappling with pain or basking in joy, connection with your Higher Self is like a force multiplier, revealing superpowers you never knew you had. Choose a practice and dive in: the more you open to it, the more synchronicities, epiphanies, miracles and magic you also let in. But the real power *behind* the power of awareness is love. All of the practices we've talked about so far – Notice, Feel, Question and Connect – are just prep work for the master practice of Love.

Because only love can really deliver a lifetime of peace and joy.

THE PRACTICES
5. Love

You yourself, as much as anyone in the universe,
deserve your love and affection.
~ Buddha

It all starts with self-love, my friend. I know that
might horrify some of you who've been trained
to put everyone and their pet hamster first, but
it's a fact. You can't love anyone else very well if
you don't love yourself first (and I mean all-out
passionately, not grudgingly or half-heartedly).
There's a reason it's a truism.

This is why we start with ourselves when
doing the Loving Kindness meditation, and if in
fact you only ever do it for yourself, you're actually
doing it for the whole world. Love recognizes that
on the level of spirit, we're all one. I am you – you
are me. As a philosophical statement it might not
be grammatically correct, but if you take it to heart
it will transform your life.

I often say it to myself when I see a homeless person/when someone cuts me off in traffic/when I feel envious of an acquaintance's good fortune/when tragedy strikes a friend. I am you – you are me. It can happen to all of us, the good and the bad. We can all be the jerk, the victim, the lucky one. Saying it is like a shortcut to the turnarounds in thought work. It's an immediate dose of humility, self-honesty, and reassurance that the human condition is unavoidable, in both its glory and its failings. Kahlil Gibran wrote: "When you reach the heart of life you will find yourself not higher than the felon, and not lower than the prophet."

And so we're going to start with loving ourselves first, and then work our way out from there. Love is a journey of discovery. Learning to love yourself necessarily means learning to know yourself better and better. Sometimes that's fun and sometimes it really isn't, so let's start with the fun stuff. We're going to figure out what things you love best and find a way for you to give yourself those things as often as possible. This is not frivolous indulgence! Rebecca West wrote: "It is the soul's duty to be loyal to its own desires." And Robert Louis Stevenson said: "To know what you prefer instead of humbly saying Amen to what the world tells you you ought to prefer, is to have kept your soul alive."

The little things that you love, and even the little things that drive you crazy for no rational reason, are like a path of breadcrumbs leading to the real you. They might seem insignificant, but they're not. So what do you love? Channel your inner Julie Andrews and make a list of your favorite things, as in: "Raindrops on roses and whiskers on kittens, bright copper kettles and warm woolen mittens…"

Consciously notice what makes your heart sing (or your teeth gnash). Make a small sacrament of the things you love. For instance, I was born on October 23rd. When I glance at a digital clock and it reads 10:23, I celebrate my "birth minute" as if it were a little wink from God. Begin to pay attention, and you'll find many of these free or inexpensive pleasures to sprinkle through your day. How about burying your nose in a bag of freshly ground coffee? Soaking in a hot bath? Reading magazines at the bookstore? Find your own sacraments and indulge in them frequently.

There's a passage I love in *The Screwtape Letters* by C.S. Lewis. The book is written from the perspective of Screwtape, a senior devil, to his nephew Wormwood, with advice on how best to tempt his "patient" into damnation. In this passage he's admonishing Wormwood for allowing his subject to enjoy a simple walk in the country. He writes: "The deepest likings and impulses of any man are the raw material, the starting point, with which the Enemy [God] has furnished him. To get him away from those is therefore always a point gained; even in things indifferent it is always desirable to substitute the standards of the World, or convention, or fashion, for a human's own real likings and dislikings."

There's an inscrutable, magical reason why we're all so unique in our tastes. Embrace the things that make you *you*. They are touchstones that will lead you to your right life. As the poet Mary Oliver wrote, all it takes is to "let the soft animal of your body love what it loves."

Bliss

Being you, living the authentic truth of who you are, is the key to happiness. Joseph Campbell famously wrote about the importance of "following your bliss." According to him, "There's something inside you that knows when you're on the beam or off the beam." As you honor what your body wants more and more, that something will grow stronger. Following your bliss isn't just about what you do for a living, but about arranging your whole life in a way that supports your authentic self, from where you live, to what you eat, to who you spend your time with.

I love personality assessments. There are many you can do free online, including the Myers-Briggs, the Enneagram, and the VIA Character Strengths assessment. Although you shouldn't define yourself or anyone else by the results, they'll give you a sense of: "Oh, yes! This is what I do/how I am" (or not). It helps to shine the flashlight of awareness on your own personality, and to marvel at the variety of responses that are possible in any given situation. One of the best gifts I ever gave my teen-age daughter was a video reading of her astrological birth chart. Now she says things like: "Well, I know I like to stay in bed because of my Taurus ascendant, but at least my Capricorn mid-heaven helps me get things done when it's important." And I didn't even pay the astrologer extra!

The poet e.e. cummings wrote: "May I be I is the only prayer – not may I be great or good or beautiful or wise or strong." This is a fundamental lesson of life. From an early age most of us are pummeled and sculpted and steamrolled into the shape that pleases our parents and teachers and friends. And then we take over the endless self-improvement project. What's needed now is not more and more, but less and less. What's needed is the courage to take off all the masks and say, "Here I am. This is the real me." Love gives you the courage to strip down to your essential self.

The irony is that, contrary to what those inner and outer voices have told us for so long, we're at our best when we're simply being ourselves. The philosopher Montaigne wrote: "The least strained and most natural ways of the soul are the most beautiful; the best occupations are the least forced." And Anne Morrow

Lindbergh remarked, "The most exhausting thing in life, I have discovered, is being insincere." I wholeheartedly agree, and I've done my best to give up insincerity for good. For me that means excusing myself from much of the typical social treadmill. Sometimes I feel a bit lonely and wallflower-ish, but it frees me up for long conversations with the people who matter to me. What feels life-sucking to you might be something entirely different. What matters is that you recognize it and have the courage to say "no" to it, and "yes" to what you love.

In any situation of stress or doubt, try asking yourself, "What's the kindest thing I can do for myself right now?" Again, this will push some major buttons for most people. We're relentlessly conditioned (especially women) to put everyone else's needs and desires first. But I absolutely know this: When I take care of my own needs, I have so much more to give to others. Repeat that twenty times a day if need be. In every moment, reach for bliss like a plant turns toward the sun. Make it a habit to check in with your body before you commit to another task or event. Don't make the Fear Choice, make the Love Choice.

Love vs. Fear

Remember that the Social Self runs on fear. Fear that you aren't "enough" on any of the endless scales we measure ourselves against. And they are endless, and you will never be on top of all of them, or even some of them, for long. The problem is, these scales are corrosive even for the people who do get to the top. And they're soul-killing for the ones who will never make it off the lower rungs. It's high school on an endless loop. Let's all boycott them, once and for all, *please*?

These patterns of behavior – comparisons, competition, and the judgments they're based on – all come from fear. Fear is the product of the reptile brain, which is all about survival. In evolutionary terms, being safely enfolded in the group provided the best chance of surviving in a hostile environment. But last time I checked, most of us are no longer living on the African savanna. (Although, come to think of it, high school might qualify as an equally hostile environment.) We don't do these things because we're mean; we do them because we're afraid. We do them because, at some point in the past, they seemed to work to keep us safe and to help us fit in.

Of course, we still want to belong. What I'm suggesting is that we become much more discerning about the people who belong to our "tribe." When you know and love and honor your authentic self, two things happen. First, you extend that same honor and love to other people in their own glorious uniqueness. And second, you begin attracting to yourself the very people who will love you for who you are. You no longer have to shimmy around to fit in with the faceless Everybody. Brené Brown, in *The Gifts of Imperfection*, calls this the "hustle for approval." It's exhausting, and in the long run it never works anyway. If you don't approve of yourself, no one else will either, unfortunately.

The practice of awareness – and holding onto yourself when you feel uncomfortable – will naturally lead to a more authentic life. Donning social masks is a front-line strategy for avoiding discomfort: The discomfort of feeling different or inadequate (judging ourselves). The discomfort of ridicule or condemnation (being judged by others). Or even just the discomfort of loneliness or boredom, which we flee into busy-ness. Fear is hands-down the most uncomfortable emotion of all. What if, instead of fleeing into your social masks, you tried breathing with that discomfort for ninety seconds?

We always have a choice of which lens to look through: fear or love. And the same situations, the same people, look completely different when we switch lenses. The compulsion to judge and condemn others that's born in fear dissolves in compassion. The poet Longfellow wrote: "If we could read the secret history of our enemies we shall find in each man's sorrow and suffering enough to disarm all hostility." The Bible got it right on this one: "Perfect love casts out fear." Compassion (or just call it kindness) toward self and others changes the whole paradigm.

No more need to "compare and despair." No need for one-up-manship. No need to judge or defend. A reign of kindness. And by kind I don't mean nice. "Nice" is a social concept that's become so watered-down, it's virtually meaningless. For a nice kid, it's enough not to bully the new student in school. A *kind* kid will sit by him at lunch. Kindness has some muscle in it. It's love in action. Seneca said, two millennia ago,

"Wherever there is a human being, there is an opportunity for a kindness."

When the Love Choice calls you out of your comfort zone and into action, it's never the kind of exhausting or life-sucking action that a Fear Choice (made from approval-seeking or a feeling of obligation) will lead you to. The feeling of a Love Choice is always expansive and joyful: check your body compass if in doubt. This is a useful way to look at any decision, but it takes careful attention to your own patterns of response. I tend to be a rescuer (did I mention that before?), frequently confusing pity with love. Many decisions I've made in the past that I thought were motivated by love were actually fear-based attempts to control my own discomfort through rescuing others. My ability to discern what's really love and what's fear has grown as I've learned to trust the messages my body sends.

Even when you can't take physical action, you can do a huge amount of good by sending the energy of love to someone in need. There's a Buddhist practice called *tonglen* in which you breathe in the pain or suffering of others, and then consciously breathe out love and healing. It's an all-purpose, anytime way to stand energetically with someone in pain, even strangers halfway across the world. Whether it's a global calamity or someone close to you who's having difficulties, worrying and suffering along in sympathy only spreads the pain further. The Sufi poet Hafiz wrote, "Troubled? Then stay with me, for I am not."

This might seem counter-intuitive or even wrong to you, but the greatest gift you can give to another, or to the world at large, is to rest in a place of peace and love yourself. Especially when they're not in that space themselves – do it "for" them. Whatever you do to or for other people, you do to and for yourself. I am you – you are me. When I love you, I'm loving myself, and when I love myself, I'm loving you. When I hate you, I'm really hating myself, and when I hate myself, I can't help but hate you on some level.

It's like we go around the world holding up giant mirrors for each other that reflect back to us what we put out. What someone else says or does is never about you; it's always about them. But how you react to them is all about you, and never about them or what they did. Everyone and everything in your world is simply a reflection of some aspect of yourself, wanted or unwanted.

When the movie of your life isn't working, you can't change it at the level of the screen... you have to look at the projector. When you change what you project into the world, I guarantee that what you see reflected back will be different.

This is both the ultimate freedom and the ultimate challenge, and I have to admit that I put up a mighty resistance to this idea for years. As much as we want to see the Shadow as something "out there" that happens to us (making us the Innocent Victim, which is really convenient and doesn't require much from us beyond finding other people to take the blame for our problems), in reality it all comes from within. The Shadow you see in others is the projection of your own Shadow, and you'll never be able to change it on the outer level if you aren't willing to own it on the inner level.

The good news is that the Shadow within is not nearly as scary as you think it is.

Loving the Shadow

What is the Shadow anyway? When the Social Self runs the show, all the ungainly, awkward, "unacceptable" parts of ourselves get shoved into the closet so that we can present an ideal façade to the world. These shadow parts are like ragged homeless children living under a bridge in our psyches. They want (and need) our attention, but we just keep pushing them back out of sight, or even trying to exterminate them. Like stuffing emotions, keeping our shadow parts hidden, from others and ourselves, requires enormous energy. Also like buried emotions, our Shadows hold important gifts and messages for us. We only have to be willing to sit down at the table with them and listen.

Your Shadow is any part of yourself that you don't fully own – both the good and the bad. What we then do is project these parts onto others in the form of admiration or aversion. Whatever attracts you to or repels you about another person is something that you also carry inside you, or it would never have caught your attention in the first place. This is great when we're talking about shadow "gold." The things you admire in others, including your heroes, are the qualities that you aspire to and which you already have in some form.

The kickback comes when we consider the qualities we hate. Of course I don't have that inside me… I would never do what (s)he does!

But here's the thing: if it's something that really grabs your attention, that has a lot of "juice" for you, there's a reason for that. Carl Jung, the king of the shadow realm, wrote, "Everything that irritates us about others can lead us to an understanding about ourselves." He also said, "To become acquainted with oneself is a terrible shock."

Have you ever noticed that something that drives you crazy might have very little effect on someone else you know? They just shrug it off, and it's probably not because they're superhuman. It's just because that isn't a trigger for them. I'm betting there are other things they hate that just don't register for you. You might not approve of them, but they don't really get under your skin.

The things that trigger you are your shadow issues. In some cases they're traits that you display yourself, but in a form that seems "harmless" to you. (When someone else makes a sarcastic remark they have anger issues, but when you do it you're just "having fun.") Sometimes it's obvious to everyone around that you have a full-blown case of the trait you're complaining about, while you remain completely blind to it. (The political ranter who abuses members of the opposing party for *their* intolerance.)

And sometimes the trait that triggers you is one that you've repressed so thoroughly that it truly doesn't show up in your own behavior… but it remains present in your Shadow, and will make itself felt over and over again in your experience until you finally acknowledge it. It wasn't until I understood this point that I truly "got it." I'll give you a personal example.

One type of behavior that has always really bugged me is "showing off," or trying to get attention. I hate this kind of "selfish" behavior, and definitely don't display it myself (cue self-righteous tone of voice). One of the pithy little phrases that life coaches like to use is: "You spot it, you got it." So when a certain person in my coach training seemed to suck up all the available attention… triggering me greatly… and a fellow student used that phrase on me, I was incensed. I definitely did NOT have that trait. In fact, I went out of my way not to "hog up" the time of our instructors or to put myself in the limelight.

You all are probably a lot faster than I was at picking up what was really going on (it's usually like that). Of course, this "selfishness" was a trait that I had vigilantly repressed from my childhood, when we were taught that it was not okay to put yourself forward or to expect any special treatment. And because I didn't allow myself to ask for any of that, I was damned sure not going to let anyone else get away with that kind of behavior. The light bulb finally came on, and with that realization I was introduced to a big piece of my shadow self. In this case it was just a little girl who wanted permission to be "special." Once I understood that, I was able to soothe her with the words she didn't hear as a child, and suddenly I found that that terribly selfish person didn't bother me nearly as much as she had. It was quite a revelation.

The scary Shadow will often turn out to be just a small, hurting child. Most of our big issues began in childhood, after all (even when you have a happy childhood and good parents... it just happens). So what do we do about the Shadow? I'm so glad you asked.

You've probably guessed the first part: just bring your awareness to it. Notice when something triggers you, when it irritates you or makes you feel mad or self-righteous. Notice what you're saying to that person (in your head, I trust) and ask yourself where you've heard that message before. Play with thought work and turnarounds to see where this behavior might be showing up in your own life. It might be obvious right away why this issue is so painful for you, or it might still be a mystery. Trust that if you're willing to receive it, you'll eventually get the insight that you need. For now all you really have to do is extend a little compassion to yourself. It's a perfect time for a Loving Kindness meditation: "May I be well. May I be happy. May I be free from suffering."

Because we're often talking about a little child here, I even like to picture myself (and the other person) as a child. Deep down, we're all really just children trying to get our needs met in the best way we know how. In fact, one simple and lovely technique to remind yourself of this is to keep a favorite picture of yourself as a child in a place where you'll see it often, and then send that child love whenever you do.

The whole point of Shadow work is to become whole again by accepting and loving even the parts of ourselves that we've considered unlovable. Pema Chödrön wrote, "We're not trying to cultivate one part of ourselves and get rid of another part. We're training in opening to it all."

And Rilke summed it up beautifully: "Perhaps everything terrible is in its deepest being something that needs our love."

Loving the Present Moment

That's the heart of the conscious, awake life in a nutshell: *Nothing is wrong.* It really is "all good," although I often find that platitude extremely annoying in the heat of the moment. The paradox of awareness is that it lets you be simultaneously right IN the moment, experiencing it deeply and personally ("mouse vision"), and at the same time to maintain the higher, compassionate and non-judgmental perspective of the Observer ("eagle vision"). It eliminates the middleman, which is the scrim of judgments, opinions, social roles, expectations, and so on that normally stands between us and our experience of what is actually happening, right here and right now.

Loving the present moment means relaxing into whatever's happening, rather than trying (futilely) to control and direct it. Or complaining constantly about it. Resistance to what is is like driving your car with the parking brake on: a waste of energy at best, and damaging if you do it often enough.

The great temptation for many people is to live most of their lives in either the past or the future (or both). Neither of them has any reality. It's true that memories can bring you joy, but stewing in regrets and simmering resentments from the past is like drinking poison again and again. Who would want that? Why contaminate this pristine moment with the worst of the past?

Even more prevalent in this culture is to live in the future. We are a goal-oriented people, driven to accomplish and to strive for change and improvement. This isn't wholly bad. The awakened life isn't just sitting around beatifically enjoying the birds and the sunshine. You can still get plenty done, and you might even be surprised by how much less effort it takes to get results when you act from the inspiration of the Higher Self rather than the directives of the ego. Inspired action seems to flow naturally, and is generally much more effective (and fun) than ego-driven action. Picture water flowing effortlessly down the path of least resistance.

The Taoist master Lao-tzu wrote, "Practice not-doing, and everything will fall into place." This will tax your ability to sit with discomfort. Usually we try to force things the most when we feel uncomfortable about something. We feel called upon to "fix it" in some way. We react reflexively to the situation, rather than taking the time to respond consciously.

So slow down and remember: *Nothing is wrong.* Whatever is happening is exactly what needs to happen in this moment. When there's something that you need to do, trust that you'll know it. In my experience, inspired action happens naturally. I find myself with the phone in my hand, or driving to the store, or doing something that I hadn't planned on, and it turns out to be exactly the thing that was needed. Stay focused on your experience of the present moment, and inspired action will result without any effort on your part at all.

I know that sounds like magic, and I guess it really is. I have to remind myself of it often. In fact, I have a card over my desk that reads, "I don't have to make anything happen." I also remind myself all the time to inhabit the moment I'm in.

This is it. This is my life, right in this moment. All I need to do is open up to all of it, with love.

In this life of today you do not live more fully than in that fleeting and transitory moment.
~ Boethius

God himself culminates in the present moment, and will never be more divine in the lapse of all the ages.
~ Thoreau

Remember then: there is only one time that is important – Now! It is the most important time because it is the only time when we have any power.
~ Tolstoy

CONCLUSION
Enlightenment 101

All of life can be integrated and assimilated into the great highway of awakening.
~ Lama Surya Das

I'm going to take a stand here: enlightenment is not just for the Buddha. Or Jesus, Mohammed, and the Dalai Lama. Or even Eckhart Tolle and Byron Katie. Enlightenment is for everyone. In fact, I'm going to go even further and say that you've already experienced moments of enlightenment. So have I. And since NOW is the only point in time with any reality, enlightenment can only be experienced in the present moment anyway. It isn't a future state to strive for, but something that can be experienced in every moment that you choose to "wake up" and be aware.

Can it really be that simple? I think so. We're all meant to wake up. The only trick is to keep making the choice in each moment to be aware, and then to string more and more of those moments together. And when you forget or "fail" to do it, that moment is already gone and you have a brand new moment in front of you to make the choice again. It's kind of beautiful, really.

I think in some ways we like to put enlightenment up on a pedestal, out of reach, because then we don't even have to *try* to realize it in our own daily lives. That's for other people, for saints and gods and mythical beings. Adyashanti wrote, "It's very hard for our minds to get that enlightenment can look like your grandmother or your grocer. It doesn't need to look in any way extraordinary... Awakening isn't about becoming extraordinary. If anything, it's about becoming ordinary. It's about becoming who we really, really are."

There's a sly irony to enlightenment that comes with being physical entities in a physical world. Imperfection and impermanence are built into this world. Even Jesus died. Even the Buddha had to eat and sleep and go to the bathroom. If enlightenment means fully accepting the present moment, then that means fully accepting impermanence and imperfection, not trying to eradicate them through force of will. Our vision of enlightenment as a kind of permanent mountaintop experience is seriously flawed.

This is just another form of spiritual by-pass. We want to turn away from all the messy bits of life and maintain a kind of hazy, Photoshopped glow of perfection, but that isn't the nature of life. "After enlightenment, the dishes," as they say. I'm advocating a kind of sturdy, feet-in-the-mud enlightenment that fully acknowledges and experiences the duality of life on Earth: hot and cold, dirty and clean, sick and well, happy and sad. It's all life, and it's all beautiful.

Some of the confusion comes from mixing up "non-attachment" with detachment. They're not the same thing! Non-attachment is learning to drop judgments of good or bad, acceptable or not acceptable, so that you can be open to your real experience of life as it's unfolding right now. In some ways it's the opposite of detachment, because the goal is to become more immersed in reality, not less.

I believe that it's all here for us. Not as an ordeal or some kind of test or performance that we have to get "right." It's more like a dance that we're creating as we go along, and the more awake we are, the more skillfully we dance (and the more we enjoy the dancing!).

We all have the Buddha consciousness (Christ consciousness) within, waiting to come out. The Buddhist teacher Chögyam Trungpa Rinpoche said, "From the perspective of doubt, whatever enlightened quality exists in us may seem small scale. From the perspective of actuality, a fully developed enlightened being exists in us already." Awareness is all that it takes to awaken the Buddha within.

So this is the end of our excursion downstream together. I feel so much gratitude for your company on the way. What's next on the journey? Maybe read a book or two, or all, from the list on the next page. These are some of the masters I look to. Make Loving Kindness meditations a regular part of your day. And here is a little exercise that recaps all of the five practices in only minutes, which I call...

The Sacred Pause

1. Take a moment to ground yourself in your physical environment. Notice what you hear, feel, smell, see and taste. Take some deep, conscious breaths.

2. Scan your body for feelings and sensations. Name them, welcome them in and see what message they have for you.

3. Notice the thoughts you're thinking (or the thoughts that have been preoccupying you that day). Ask yourself: Are they true?

4. Make a conscious connection with something bigger than yourself: God, nature, the Universe, your Higher Self, Christ consciousness. Picture this loving energy flooding into you.

5. Now turn that energy out into the world. Send love and gratitude to your Source

and to all people, plants, animals and the world around you.

And above all, be gentle with yourself.

For being human, we remember and forget. We stray and return, fall down and get up, and cling and let go, again and again. But it is this straying and returning that makes life interesting, this clinging and letting go – damned as it is – that exercises the heart.
~ Mark Nepo

RECOMMENDED READING (a beginning!)

Martha Beck: *The Joy Diet, Finding Your Own North Star* (basically anything)

Byron Katie: *Loving What Is*

Eckhart Tolle: *The Power of Now*

Esther and Jerry Hicks: *Ask and It Is Given*

Tosha Silver: *Outrageous Openness*

Rob Bell: *What We Talk About When We Talk About God*

Russ Harris: *The Happiness Trap*

Pema Chödrön: *When Things Fall Apart*

Brooke Castillo: *Self Coaching 101*

Brené Brown: *The Gifts of Imperfection*

Debbie Ford: *The Dark Side of the Light Chasers*

Jon Kabat-Zinn: *Mindfulness for Beginners*

Karla McLaren: *The Language of Emotions*

Marci Shimoff: *Happy for No Reason*

Adyashanti: *True Meditation: Discover the Freedom of Pure Awareness*

ABOUT THE AUTHOR

Amaya Pryce is a writer, writing coach and editor who lives with her daughter and cats in the Pacific Northwest.

She blogs at: www.professionalstudentoflife.com

Photo by Phyllis Lane: www.phyllislane.com

Made in the USA
Middletown, DE
29 May 2016